Introductic

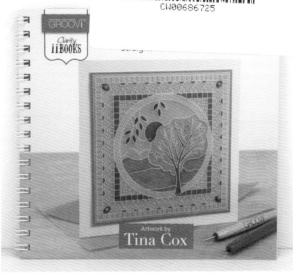

Once you get into Parchment Craft, you soon want to master that fabulous lacework which parchers so often use to frame their artwork. Done traditionally, this requires lots of counting (and focus!), but Tina has developed a brilliant series of Border Pattern Grids, both straight and diagonal, to help you create beautiful gridwork and lacework easily.

Previously we published a series of Tina Cox's *Parchment Perforating Guides,* written to accompany her clever and innovative *Border Pattern Grids.* The first books cover the basics of creating patterns utilising the straight and diagonal grids. Be sure to check out the *'Parchment Perforating Guide - Straight Border Pattern Grid no1'* (ACC-BO-30456-XX) baefore progressing to this book. It's not a strict necessity to do so, but I'd recommend it.

In this *ADVANCED GUIDE* we introduce the technique of picot cutting the perforations you can make with the straight grid. Without too much trouble and with the help of the grid patterns as a guide, you too will be creating masterful intricate lacework with relative ease!

Enjoy the picot trail!
Barbara Gray

Tools & Items Used In This Book

Clarity Lightwave (ACC-LP-30352-A4)
Regular parchment paper (GRO-AC-40020-XX)
Purple parchment paper (GRO-AC-40189-A5)
Blue parchment paper (GRO-AC-40190-A5)
A4 Translucent Piercing Mat (GRO-AC-40307-A4)
A4 Translucent White Super Foam (GRO-AC-40603-A4)
Pergamano Excellent Embossing Mat (PER-AC-70075-XX)
A4 Picot Foam (GRO-AC-40625-XX)
Groovi Plate Starter Kit (GRO-SK-40571-XX)
Groovi Border Plate Mate (GRO-MA-40348-13)
Groovi Calligraphy Alphabet A5 Groovi Plate Mate (GRO-MA-40517-08)
Groovi A6 Inset (GRO-WO-40133-11)
Border Pattern Grid Straight No. 1 (GRO-GG-40350-14)
Straight Basic Piercing Grid (GRO-GG-40202-12)
Pergamano Bold 1-needle perforating tool (PER-TO-70028-XX)
Pergamano Bold 2-needle perforating tool (PER-TO-70279-XX)
Pergamano Fine 2-needle perforating tool (PER-TO-70037-XX)
Pergamano scissors exclusive (PER-TO-70040-XX)
Pergamano 0.5mm Stylus (PER-TO-70010-XX)
Pergamano 1mm ball tool (PER-TO-70012-XX)
Pergamano 1.5mm ball tool (PER-TO-70004-XX)
Pergamano 3mm ball tool (PER-TO-70005-XX)
Pergamano 4.5mm ball tool (PER-TO-70015-XX)
Pergamano Shader tool 1mm (PER-TO-70002-XX)
Pergamano Shader tool 1.2mm (PER-TO-70003-XX)
Pergamano mapping pen (PER-TO-70039-XX)
Perga Glitter (PER-AC-70252-XX)
Perga Liners (PER-CO-70063-XX)
Pergamano Dorso oil (PER-CO-70066-XX)
Perga Colours Exclusive (PER-CO-70060-XX)
Groovi Guard (GRO-AC-40345-XX)
Groovi Sticker Tabs (GRO-AC-40437-XX)
Sweet Dreams Designer Paper 8"x8" (ACC-CA-30442-88)
Indian Summer Designer Paper 8"x8" (ACC-CA-30524-88)
Sticky Ink (PER-AC-70134-XX)

The Grid

This Border Pattern Grid comprises five basic patterns.

These pattern grids can be used to emboss or perforate.
Emboss from the back and perforate from the front of your parchment.

This book will also show you how to use these patterns to picot cut your perforations to make beautiful and intricate cut outs.

Perforated & Embossed

Here we see each of the 5 patterns either embossed or perforated along a straight line, just as they come on the pattern grid.
You can also combine embossing and perforating to produce beautiful lacework. See instructions below and overleaf.
If you plan to perforate and emboss, it is good practice to wipe the front and back of your parchment with a tumble dryer sheet before you begin.

Perforating & Embossing

COMBINED

1. If starting with embossing
a. Attach parchment onto the pattern grid, back facing up.
b. Emboss pattern with No. 2 ball tool from Groovi Starter Kit, or 1.5mm Pergamano ball tool.
c. Remove from grid.
d. Turn parchment over (front), line up embossed dots on straight basic grid & attach.
e. Perforate design between embossed dots using 1-needle bold tool.

2. If starting with perforating
a. Attach parchment onto the pattern grid, front facing up.
b. Perforate pattern with 1-needle bold tool.
c. Remove from grid.
d. Turn parchment over (back facing up), line up perforated holes on straight basic grid and attach.
e. Emboss the design between the perforated holes, again using the No. 2 or the 1.5mm ball tool.

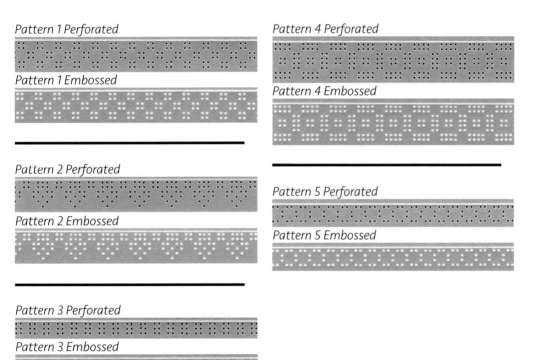

Pattern 1 Perforated

Pattern 1 Embossed

Pattern 2 Perforated

Pattern 2 Embossed

Pattern 3 Perforated

Pattern 3 Embossed

Pattern 4 Perforated

Pattern 4 Embossed

Pattern 5 Perforated

Pattern 5 Embossed

Picot Cutting a Line

One of the most important skills to learn when mastering the art of parchment craft is cutting. A good cut is all about cutting the connections between each perforation, to ensure a neat, even picot point. For the purpose of this book we are going to concentrate on perforations made with the aid of a Groovi Grid.

● *Perforation*　　● *Cut line*

1. Place your parchment on a Straight Basic Grid and secure with Groovi Tabs to stop the parchment from sliding around. Now you are ready to perforate. Don't forget to perforate on top of a perforating mat to protect your work surface.

2. Perforate a straight line using a Straight Basic Grid.

3. When you have finished perforating you can start cutting your picot edge. During cutting you need to make sure that the waste parchment i.e. the parchment that you are cutting away, is always positioned underneath the blades of your scissors when the points are inserted into the perforations.

4. Hold the scissors with the curved end pointing downward. Put your right index finger in the left hole of the scissors and your middle finger in the right hole of the scissors. Brace your thumb against the outside of the left hole of the scissors. If you are left-handed place the index finger of your left hand in the right hole of the scissors and the middle finger in the left hole. Holding your scissors in this way may feel a little alien at first, but this is the conventional and most used way. There are numerous other ways, too many to mention, but try and find the most comfortable way that suits you. You could also try using the scissors with the curved end pointing upwards, whichever gives you the best results.

5. Now insert the points of the scissors (not too deeply) into the two perforations that are nearest to you.

6. Next, tilt the scissors down toward the paper as much as possible without removing the tips from the perforations. The scissors should be almost parallel to the paper.

7. Start the cutting motion and cut the connection between the perforations, tilting your hand and the scissors slightly towards you as you snip. You will hear a snapping noise each time you cut. A small point will be created between the perforations after each cut. Now move along the line of holes cutting as you go.

Picot Cutting a Cross

1. Place your parchment on a Straight Border Pattern Grid No 1 and secure with Groovi Tabs to stop the parchment from sliding around. Now perforate the first two lines of the grid (Pattern 1) which will give you a line of clusters of four perforations (much like the diagram across). Don't forget to perforate on top of a perforating mat to protect your work surface.

2. In the diagram across we have numbered the holes of the perforation so you can follow the rotations you will need to perform to achieve the cross technique. Now place the points of your scissors into perforations 1 and 2. Lower your scissors so that it is almost parallel to the parchment paper. Now make your first cut, tilting your scissors very slightly towards you as you do so. This should form a neat point known as a picot.

3. Turn your parchment a quarter turn to the left so that holes 2 and 3 are uppermost and repeat the cutting process.

4. Turn the parchment a quarter turn to the left again, so that holes 3 and 4 are uppermost and cut as before.

5. Turn the parchment for the last time so that holes 4 and 1 are now uppermost, and make your final cut. At this stage the centre should fall out leaving a neat cross shape.

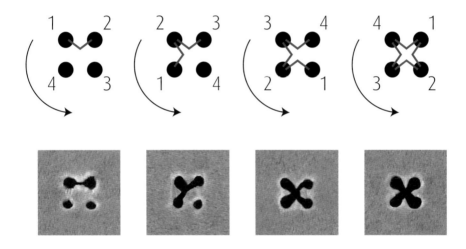

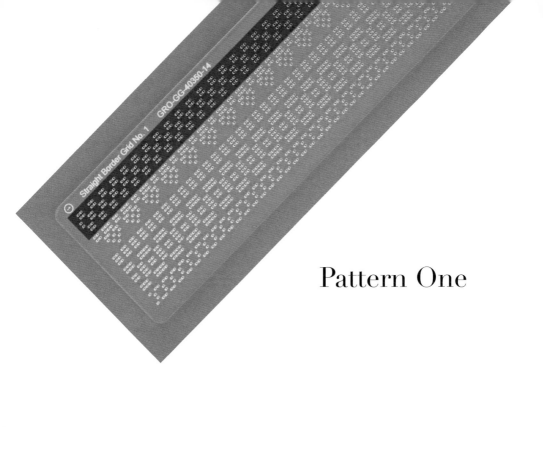

Pattern One

Pattern One - Perforated, Embossed & Cut

A QUICK HOW-TO USING PATTERN 1

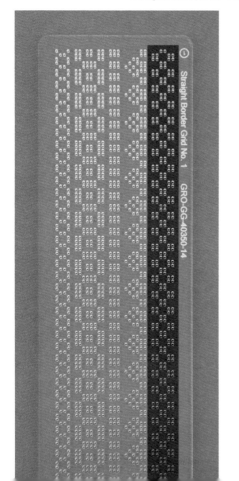

Example 1a

1. Perforate one row of border pattern 1.

2. Turn the parchment over and emboss dots over the basic straight grid.

3. Turn the parchment to the front and picot cut.

Example 1b

1. Perforate the border pattern 1.

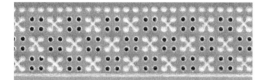

2. Turn the parchment over and emboss dots over the basic grid straight and freehand emboss lines between the dots using a 0.5mm ball tool.

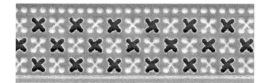

3. Turn the parchment to the front and picot cut.

Example 1c

1. Perforate two rows of border pattern 1.

2. Turn the parchment over and freehand emboss circles between the bottom row of perforations using a 1.5mm ball tool.

3. Turn the parchment to the front and picot cut.

Floral Mandala

DESIGNED USING PATTERN 1

Ingredients

Groovi Grids: *Straight Border Pattern Grid No.1, Straight Basic Border*
Groovi Plate Mates: *Alphabet A5², Art Deco Alphabet Border*
Groovi A5² Plates: *Nested squares*
Groovi A4 Plates: *Tina's Henna Corners 2*

To Make

1. Emboss the 3rd, 4th, 6th and 7th squares from the outside of the nested square plate.

2. Emboss the rest of the designs from the plates.

3. Freehand emboss inside the henna flower design.

4. Colour on the back with Perga Colours Exclusive.

5. Perforate, emboss and cut the border pattern 1a inside the double outlined squares.

6. Trim back the piece of work and mount onto purple parchment and designer paper (I've used a sheet from the 'Sweet Dreams' designer paper pack) using brads and attach to a 6"x6" card blank.

Domed Dahlia

DESIGNED USING PATTERN 1

Ingredients

Groovi Grids: *Straight Border Pattern Grid No.1, Straight Basic Border, Straight Basic A5²*

Groovi Plate Mates: *Calligraphy Alphabet A5, Alphabet A5, Art Deco Alphabet Border*

Groovi A5² Plates: *Nested Squares, Jayne's Dahlias Name*

Groovi A5 Plates: *Nested Tags*

To Make

1. Emboss 2nd and 3rd squares from the outside of the nested square plate.

2. Perforate and emboss the border pattern 1b about half way down inside the square.

3. Perforate and emboss the border pattern 1b inside the double outlined square and freehand emboss lines between the dots using a 0.5mm tool.

4. Emboss the dahlia and the 2nd from outside nested tag.

5. Add faint texture in the tag by rubbing the Groovi no.4 ball tool followed by the no.3 ball tool over the basic straight grid.

6. Colour on the back with Perga Colours Exclusive.

7. Cut between all the perforations.

8. Trim back the piece of work and mount it on purple parchment using brads and attach to a 6"x6" card blank.

Countryside Christmas

Ingredients

Groovi Grids: *Straight Border Pattern Grid No.1, Straight Basic Border.*
Groovi Plate Mates: *Alphabet A5², Art Deco Alphabet Border*
Groovi A5² Plates: *Nested Squares*
Groovi A4 Plates: *Jayne's Winter Scene - Cat, Tina's Christmas Corners 2*

To Make

1. Emboss 3rd from the outside square and turn parchment to emboss double outlines at a diagonal using the 1st and 3rd squares from the outside.

2. Emboss the rest of the designs from the plates.

3. Add white work where required on the design.

4. Colour on the back with Perga Liner B pencils and blend with Dorso oil.

5. Perforate, emboss and cut the border pattern 1b inside the double outlined squares.

6. Mount the piece of work on purple parchment and designer paper (from 'Sweet Dreams' designer paper pack) using brads and attach to a 6"x6" card blank.

7. Add a little sparkle using sticky ink, mapping pen and hint of silver Perga glitter.

Pattern Two

Pattern Two - Perforated, Embossed & Cut

A QUICK HOW-TO USING PATTERN 2

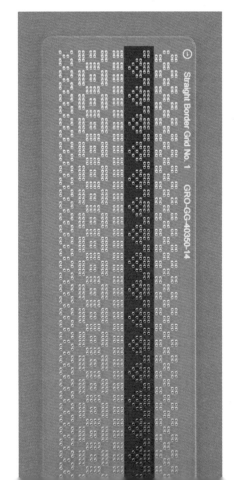

Straight Border Grid No. 1 GRO-GG-40350-14

Example 2a

1. Perforate border pattern 2.

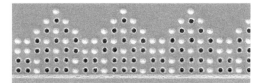

2. Turn the parchment over and emboss dots over the basic grid straight.

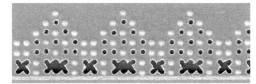

3. Turn the parchment to the front and picot cut.

Example 2b

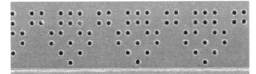

1. Perforate border pattern 2.

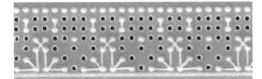

2. Turn the parchment over and emboss dots over the basic grid straight and freehand emboss lines between the dots using a 0.5mm ball tool.

3. Turn the parchment to the front and picot cut.

Example 2c

1. Perforate border pattern 2.

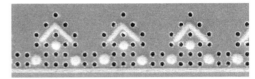

2. Turn the parchment over and freehand emboss circles and lines using 1mm and 1.5mm ball tools.

3. Turn the parchment to the front and picot cut.

Delicate Deco Poppies

DESIGNED USING PATTERN 2

Ingredients

Groovi Grids: *Straight Border Pattern Grid No.1, Straight Basic Border, Diagonal Basic A5².*

Groovi Plate Mates: *Alphabet A5², Art Deco Alphabet Border*

Groovi A5² Plates: *Nested Scallops Squares, Nested Circles, Sprig Background, Art Nouveau Poppies.*

To Make

1. Emboss 1st scallop and squares from the outside of the scallop nested squares and the 5th from outside circle on the bottom left corner.

2. Perforate and emboss the border pattern 2a on the inside of the square.

3. Emboss the rest of the designs from the plates.

4. Freehand emboss in the leaves.

5. Emboss dots between the double circles over the basic grid diagonal.

6. On the back, using Perga Colours Exclusive, paint the poppies, stems, leaves and scallops. Colour and blend using Perga Liner B pencils and Dorso oil in the circles.

7. Perforate outside the scallops using a 2-needle bold perforating tool and picot cut between all the perforations.

8. Mount the piece of work on blue parchment using brads and attach to a 6" x 6" card blank.

Woven Florals

Ingredients

Groovi Grids: *Straight Border Pattern Grid No.1, Straight Basic Border, Straight Basic A5 Grid.*
Groovi A5² Plates: *Nested Squares, Woven Background, Floral Moon.*
Groovi A6² Plates: *Flowers and Vases.*
Groovi Plate Mates: *Alphabet A5², Art Deco Alphabet Border, A6 Inset.*

To Make

1. Emboss the 3rd and 7th squares from the outside

2. Emboss the rest of the designs from the plates.

3. Add white work to the inside the flower petals.

4. Emboss dots in the corners between the circle and square and in the vases.

5. Colour on the back using Perga Colours Exclusive in the vases and woven background and inside the circle use Perga Liner B pencils and blend with Dorso oil.

6. Perforate, emboss and cut the border pattern 2b outside the large square.

7. Trim back the piece of work and mount it on blue parchment and white card using brads and attach to a 6" x 6" card blank.

Welcome Bouquet

DESIGNED USING PATTERN 2

Ingredients

Groovi Grids: *Straight Border Pattern Grid No.1, Straight Basic A5 Grid, Straight Basic Border Grid*
Groovi A6 Plates: *Welcome Framer*
Groovi A5² Plates: *Nested Squares*
Groovi Plate Mates: *Alphabet A5², Art Deco Alphabet Border*
Groovi Spacer Plates: *Spacer 1*

To Make

1. Emboss the 'Welcome' design.

2. Emboss part of the 1st square from the outside to form into a rectangle.

3. Emboss dots over the basic grid straight in the letter 'O'

4. Colour on the back using Perga Colours Exclusive.

5. Perforate and emboss the border pattern 2c on the bottom side of the frame.

6. Perforate outside the other 3 sides of the rectangle using a bold 2-needle perforating tool and cut between all the perforations.

7. Attach your piece of work to blue parchment using brads and then tear the bottom edge at a slight angle. Attach a piece of purple parchment to the lower part of a 6" x 6" card blank and then attach your design.

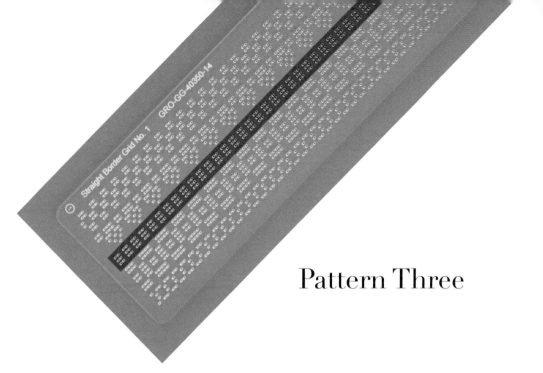

Pattern Three

33

Pattern Three - Perforated, Embossed & Cut

A QUICK HOW-TO USING PATTERN 3

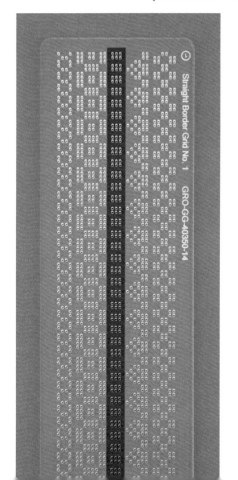

Example 3a

1. Perforate border pattern 3

2. Turn the parchment over and emboss dots over the straight basic grid.

3. Turn the parchment to the front and picot cut

Example 3b

1. Emboss border pattern 3 and freehand emboss lines between the dots using a 0.5 ball tool.

2. Turn the parchment over and perforate the holes over the basic straight grid.

3. Picot cut.

Example 3c

1. Perforate border pattern 3.

2. Perforate extra holes between the border pattern over the basic straight grid.

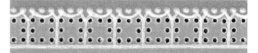

3. Turn the parchment over and emboss dots over the basic straight grid and freehand emboss lines and scallops between the dots using a 0.5 ball tool.

4. Turn the parchment to the front and picot cut.

Forever Friends

Ingredients

Groovi Grids: *Straight Border Pattern Grid No.1, Straight Basic A5 Grid, Diagonal Basic A5 Grid*
Groovi Plate Mates: *Alphabet A5², Art Deco Alphabet Border, Calligraphy Alphabet A5 Plate.*
Groovi A5² Plates: *Nested Squares, Nested Scallops Circles, Leafy Swirl*
Groovi A5 Plates: *If I Had A Flower.*
Groovi Border Plates: *Gratitude and Sending Hugs Word Chain Border.*

To Make

1. Emboss 2nd and 3rd squares from the outside of the nested squares and in the middle, emboss the 4th circles from the outside of the nested scallop circles.

2. Emboss the rest of the designs from the plates.

3. Freehand emboss the birds.

4. Emboss dots from the basic diagonal plate inside the leaves.

5. Colour on the back with Perga Liner B pencils and blend with Dorso oil. Use the grey Perga Colour Exclusive pen to colour the word, circle frame, inside flower petals and small squares.

6. Perforate, emboss and cut the border pattern 3a outside the main square.

7. Trim back the piece of work and mount onto purple parchment using brads and attach to a 6" x 6" card blank.

Winter Greetings

DESIGNED USING PATTERN 3

Ingredients

Groovi Grids: *Straight Border Pattern Grid No.1, Straight Basic Border Grid, Diagonal Basic A5.*
Groovi A4² Plates: *Tina's Christmas Corners 1.*
Groovi A5² Plates: *Nested Squares.*
Groovi Plate Mates: *Alphabet A5², Art Deco Alphabet Border.*
Groovi Border Plate: *Christmas Word Chains Plate.*

To Make

1. Emboss the 3rd square from the outside of the nested squares.

2. Emboss the rest of the designs from the plates.

3. Add some whitework to the bow and bell.

4. Emboss dots using the basic diagonal grid inside the bell and heart.

5. Colour on the back using Perga Colours Exlcusive.

6. Emboss, perforate and cut the border pattern 3b outside the main square.

7. Attach the piece to purple parchment and designer paper using brads and attach to a 6" x 6" card blank..

8. Add a little sparkle using sticky ink, a mapping pen and hint of blue Perga Glitter.

Best Wishes

A Symphony of Wishes

DESIGNED USING PATTERN 3

Ingredients

Groovi Grids: *Straight Border Pattern Grid No.1, Straight Basic Border Grid.*
Groovi Plate Mate: *Alphabet A5², Art Deco Alphabet Border.*
Groovi A5² Plates: *Nested Squares, Musical Instruments, Musical Score.*
Groovi Border Plate: *Occasions.*

To Make

1. Emboss the 2nd and 3rd squares from the outside of the nested squares.

2. Emboss the rest of the designs from the plates.

3. Colour on the back with Perga Liner B pencils and blend with Dorso oil.

4. Between the double square outlines, emboss the border pattern 3b and freehand emboss lines between the dots using a 0.5 ball tool.

5. Perforate, emboss and cut the border pattern 3c outside the main square.

6. Trim back the piece of work and mount it on purple parchment using brads and attach to a 6" x 6" card blank.

Pattern Four

Pattern Four - Perforated, Embossed & Cut

A QUICK HOW-TO USING PATTERN 4

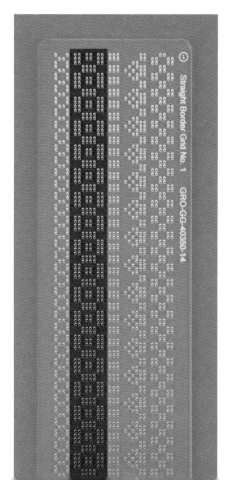

Example 4a

1. Perforate border pattern 4.

2. Turn the parchment over emboss dots over the basic straight grid.

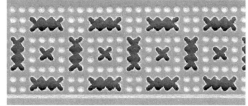

3. Turn the parchment to the front and picot cut.

Example 4b

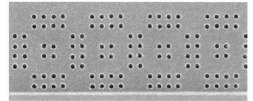

1. Perforate border pattern 4.

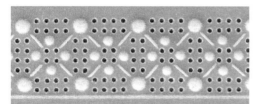

2. Turn the parchment over and freehand emboss circles using 1 and 1.5 ball tools and lines using a 0.5 ball tool.

3. Turn the parchment to the front and picot cut .

Example 4c

1. Perforate border pattern 4.

2. Turn the parchment over and freehand emboss circles and squares using 1 and 1.5 ball tools.

3. Turn the parchment to the front and picot cut.

45

GROOVI

Delicate Daisies

Ingredients

Groovi Grids: *Straight Border Pattern Grid No.1, Straight Basic Border.*
Groovi Plate Mate: *Alphabet A5², Art Deco Alphabet Border, A6 Inset*
Groovi A5² Plates: *Nested Squares*
Groovi A6 Plates: *Thank you Framer, Art Deco Lady Baby Plate.*
Groovi A4 Plates: *Tina's 3D Flowers & Butterflies*
Groovi Spacer Plates: *Spacer 1*

To Make

1. Emboss the 4th square from the outside of the nested squares.

2. Perforate and emboss border pattern 4a diagonally inside the frame.

3. Emboss the rest of the designs from the plates.

4. Following the curve of the frame, emboss the dots over the straight border piercing grid, along the stems and in the butterfly wings.

5. Paint on the back using Perga Colours Exclusive.

6. Perforate and emboss the border pattern 4a outside the main square.

7. In the corners, emboss part of the flower petal from the flower plate.

8. Cut between all the perforations.

9. Trim back the piece of work and mount onto blue parchment using brads and attach to a 6" x 6" card blank.

A Fairy Wish

DESIGNED USING PATTERN 4

Ingredients

Groovi Grids: *Straight Border Pattern Grid No.1, Straight Basic Border Grid*
Groovi Plate Mate: *Alphabet A5², Art Deco Alphabet Border*
Groovi A5² Plates: *Nested Squares*
Groovi A6 Plates: *Fairy 2*
Groovi Spacer Plates: *Welcome Plaque Spacer, Balance Spacer*

To Make

1. Emboss the 3rd square from the outside of the nested square.s

2. Emboss the rest of the designs from the plates.

3. Add some white work to parts of the design.

4. On the back, colour the inside of the tag, wings, hands, legs and face with Perga Liner B pencils and blend with Dorso oil. Colour the fairy outfit, hair, flowers and leaves and between tag frame with Perga Colours Exclusive.

5. Perforate, emboss and cut the border pattern 4b outside the main square.

6. Trim back the piece of work and mount it on blue parchment using brads and attach to a 6" x 6" card blank..

7. Add a little sparkle using sticky ink, mapping pen and hint of pink Perga Glitter.

Sunny Scenic Panels

DESIGNED USING PATTERN 4

Ingredients

Groovi Grids: *Straight Border Pattern Grid No.1, Straight Basic Border, Straight Basic A5*

Groovi Plate Mate: *Alphabet A5², Art Deco Alphabet Border, Calligraphy Alphabet A5*

Groovi A5² Plates: *Nested Squares*

Groovi A5 Plates: *Nested Rectangles, Sunbeam Moonbeam, Today Well Lived.*

Groovi A4 Plates: *Landscape & Skylines*

To Make

1. Emboss 3 sides of the 3rd square from outside of the nested squares plate and the 3rd and 2nd rectangles from the inside of the nested rectangles plate.

2. Emboss the rest of the designs from the plates.

3. Emboss dots around the rectangles using the straight basic grid.

4. Colour on the back with Perga Liner B pencils and blend with Dorso oil.

5. Perforate and emboss the border pattern 4c on the bottom of the square.

6. Using the bold 2-needle perforating tool, perforate outside the other 3 sides of the square and picot cut between all the perforations.

7. Mount the piece of work on blue parchment and designer paper using brads and attach to a 6″ x 6″ card blank.

Pattern Five

Pattern Five - Perforated, Embossed & Cut

A QUICK HOW-TO USING PATTERN 5

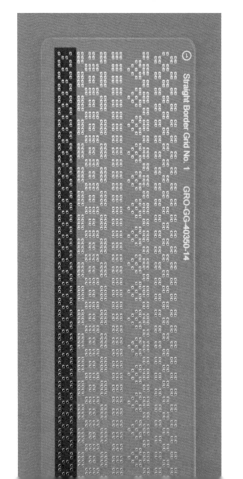

Example 5a

1. Emboss border pattern 5.

2. Turn the parchment over and perforate using the basic straight grid.

3. Turn the parchment to the front and picot cut.

Example 5b

1. Perforate border pattern 5.

2. Turn the parchment over and freehand emboss circles using a 1.5mm ball tool.

3. Turn the parchment to the front and picot cut.

Example 5c

1. Perforate border pattern 5.

2. Turn the parchment over and emboss dots over the basic straight grid and freehand emboss lines between the dots using a 0.5 ball tool.

3. Turn the parchment to the front and picot cut.

Winter Foliage

DESIGNED USING PATTERN 5

Ingredients

Groovi Grids: *Straight Border Pattern Grid No.1, Straight Basic Border*
Groovi Plate Mate: *Alphabet A5², Art Deco Alphabet Border*
Groovi A5² Plates: *Nested Scallops Squares*
Groovi A4 Plates: *Tina's Christmas Corners 2 & 4*

To Make

1. Emboss the 3rd, 6th, 11th and 14th squares from the outside of the nested scallop squares and the scallops outside the 3rd square.

2. Emboss the rest of the designs from the plates.

3. Add white work to the snowflakes.

4. On the back, colour the poinsettia, stars, hearts and scallops with Perga Colours Exclusive and inside the double square outlines with Perga Liner B pencils and blend with Dorso oil.

5. Emboss and perforate the border pattern 5a inside the double square outlines.

6. Perforate between the poinsettia and outside the scallops with the bold 2-needle perforating tool and picot cut between all the perforations.

7. Mount the piece of work on purple parchment and designer paper using brads and attach to a 6" x 6" card blank.

8. Add a little sparkle using sticky ink, mapping pen and hint of pink Perga glitter.

Fantasy Fuchsias

DESIGNED USING PATTERN 5

Ingredients

Groovi Grids: *Straight Border Pattern Grid No.1, Straight Basic Border, Straight Basic A5*
Groovi Plate Mate: *Alphabet A5², Art Deco Alphabet Border*
Groovi A5² Plates: *Nested Squares, Nested Circles, Jayne's Fuchsias*
Groovi A4 Plates: *Tina's Floral Swirls and Corners 1*

To Make

1. Emboss the 4th square from the outside of the nested squares and the 7th circle from the outside of the nested circles.

2. Emboss the rest of the designs from the plates.

3. Emboss dots using a basic straight grid and freehand emboss lines between the dots using a 0.5 ball tool to create the background.

4. Colour on the back with Perga Liner B pencils and blend with Dorso oil.

5. Perforate, emboss and cut the pattern around the circle and the border pattern 5b outside the main square.

6. Trim back the piece of work and mount onto purple parchment using brads and attach to a 6" x 6" card blank..

A Pocket of Time

DESIGNED USING PATTERN 5

Ingredients

Groovi Grids: *Straight Border Pattern Grid No.1, Straight Basic Border*
Groovi Plate Mate: *Alphabet A5², Art Deco Alphabet Border*
Groovi A5² Plates: *Nested Squares, Nested Circles, Netting Pattern, Clocks*
Groovi Border Plates: *My Art Word Chain, Arrows, Gratitude & Sending Hugs*

To Make

1. Emboss the 4th square from the outside of the nested squares.

2. Emboss the rest of the designs from the plates (NB I have used the 5th circle from the outside of the nested circles plate.

3. Colour on the back with Perga Liner B pencils and blend with Dorso oil.

4. Perforate and emboss the border pattern 5c outside the main square.

5. Perforate with the bold 2-needle perforating tool inside the netting and picot cut between all the perforations.

6. Mount the piece of work on purple parchment and white card using brads and attach to a 6" x 6" card blank..

The **Big** Project

Dream Big

Now let's put our knowledge to the test and put our new skills into practice. This time using all of the patterns as they appear on the Straight Border Pattern Grid No. 1, directly into a project.

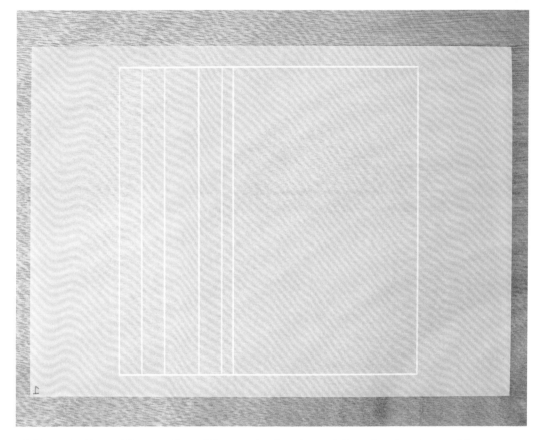

1. From the Nested Squares Groovi Plate and using the no.1 Groovi embossing tool (or Pergamano 1mm), emboss the 1st square from the outside.

On the left hand side of the square, emboss lines from top to bottom using the 3rd, 5th, 8th, 10th and 11th squares from the outside as guides

2. Emboss the rest of the design on the parchment from the Dream Dangles Groovi Plate.

3. **Still working on the back of our work,** use Perga Liner B pencils and Dorso oil to blend, colour alternate strips as show above.

Next, using the Perga Colour pens, colour the dream catcher and dangles design.

4. **Working** on the front, perforate each of the designs as shown above using a Pergamano bold 1-needle perforating tool.

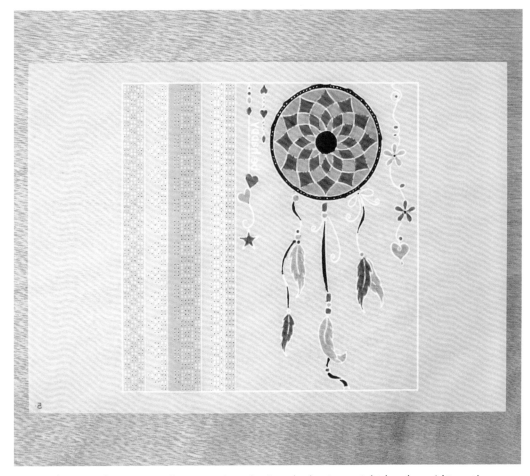

5. Working on the reverse of your work and using the basic staright border grid together with the Groovi No2 embossing tool (or Pergamano 1.5mm), emboss dots between the pattern perforations as shown.

6.

6. **Working on the** front, use a Pergamano bold 2-needle perforating tool, perforate between the pattern grid work and lines between the slots. Then perforate around the outside of the main square.

Picot cut between all the perforations using Pergamano scissors or Perga Cutters.

To Finish: Mount the work on purple parchment and black card using brads. Layer onto a piece of Indian Summer Designer Paper or Parchment and then attach to a 7" x 7" card blank.

Index Of Groovi Plates Used

A4 Square Plates:

Landscapes & Skylines - GRO-LA-40669-15
Henna Corners 2 - GRO-FL-40663-15
Jayne's Winter Scene - Cat - GRO-WI-40450-15
Tina's Christmas Corners 2 - GRO-CH-40697-15
Tina's Christmas Corners 1 - GRO-CH-40696-15
Tina's 3D Flowers & Butterflies - GRO-FL-40553-15

A5 Square Pates:

Nested Squares - GRO-PA-40037-03
Jayne's Dahlias - GRO-FL-40411-03
Nested Scallops Squares - GRO-PA-40557-03
Neste Circles - GRO-PA-40051-03
Sprig Background - GRO-FL-40008-03
Art Nouveau Poppies - GRO-FL-40123-10
Woven Background - GRO-PA-40097-03
Floral Moon - GRO-FL-40446-03
Leafy Swirl - GRO-TR-40338-03
Musical Instruments - GRO-MU-40204-03

A5 Plates:

Today Well Lived - GRO-WO-40624-04
Sunbeam Moonbeam - GRO-WO-40521-04
Nested Rectangles - GRO-PA-40524-04
If I Had a Flower - GRO-WO-40604-04

A6 Square Plates:

Flowers & Vases - GRO-FL-40335-01
Art Deco Lady - GRO-PE-40178-01

A6 Plates:

Welcome Framer - GRO-WO-40685-02
Thank You Framer - GRO-WO-40598-02
Fairy 2 - GRO-FY-40709-02

Border Plates:

Gratitude and Sending Hugs - GRO-WO-40564-09
Christmas Word Chains - GRO-WO-40566-09
Occasions - GRO-WO-40060-09

Spacers Plates:

Spacer 1 - GRO-MA-40623-06
Welcome Plaque - GRO-WO-40684-06
Balance - GRO-WO-40655-06